Wissler, Clark, 1870-1947.

COSTUMES OF THE PLAINS INDIANS

together with

STRUCTURAL BASIS TO THE DECORATION OF COSTUMES AMONG THE PLAINS INDIANS

AMS PRESS
NEW YORK

ANTHROPOLOGICAL PAPERS

OF

THE AMERICAN MUSEUM OF NATURAL HISTORY

VOL. XVII, PART II

—

COSTUMES OF THE PLAINS INDIANS

⌐ BY

CLARK WISSLER ⌐.

NEW YORK
PUBLISHED BY ORDER OF THE TRUSTEES
1915

Library of Congress Cataloging in Publication Data

Wissler, Clark, 1870-1947.
 Costumes of the Plains Indians & Structural
basis to the decoration of costumes among the
Plains Indians.

 Reprint of the 1915 and 1916 editions published
by order of the Trustees of the American Museum
of Natural History, New York, which were issued as
v. 17, pt. 2 and v. 17, pt. 3 of the Museum's
Anthropological papers, respectively.
 1. Indians of North America—Great Plains—Costume
and adornment. I. Wissler, Clark, 1870-1947. Structural
basis to the decoration of costumes among the Plains
Indians. 1975. II. Title: Costumes of the Plains Indians. . . .
III. Series: American Museum of Natural History, New
York. Anthropological papers; v. 17, pts. 2-3.
E78.G73W56   1975   391   74-9016
ISBN 0-404-11913-1

Reprinted from the edition of 1915-1916, New York
First AMS edition published in 1975.
Manufactured in the United States of America

AMS PRESS INC.
NEW YORK, N. Y. 10003

COSTUMES OF THE PLAINS INDIANS.

BY CLARK WISSLER.

PREFACE.

The following study has as its chief object not so much the mere descriptions of certain types of garments among the Indians of the Plains as the presentation of a typical trait in material culture and the development of the problems involved. In a former paper on the *Material Culture of the Blackfoot Indians* some attention was given to the forms and distributions of men's shirts and women's dresses in order to determine the place of Blackfoot culture in the Plains group. This paper presents some of the results obtained by a far more intensive study of specimens from the Plains area as a whole. The specimens described are from the Museum's collections, particularly from the collection presented by J. P. Morgan in 1910; but the writer is under obligation to Dr. Walter Hough of the United States National Museum, A. C. Parker of the New York State Museum, C. C. Willoughby of the Peabody Museum at Cambridge, and to Dr. Fay Cooper Cole of the Field Museum of Natural History for equally important data from their respective institutions.

The structural analysis of the specimens was largely the work of my assistant, Mr. S. Ichikawa, who is to that extent a joint contributor. The drawings should also be credited to him.

August, 1915.

CONTENTS.

ILLUSTRATIONS.

TEXT FIGURES.

INTRODUCTION.

The anthropological literature of some years ago gave considerable attention to problems in the development of industrial processes. The genetic relation of inventions as traits of culture were sought in a more or less world wide objective comparison. The order of the method was to retrace by logical analysis the steps by which a given technical process was developed. Thus, such arts as fire-making, stone chipping, pottery, etc., were intensively studied and their more complex forms analyzed to seek for the elemental or beginning processes, with the idea of ultimately reconstructing the evolution, or history, of each. Some years ago such studies were energetically pursued and consequently occupy a large place in the literature of that time. They finally came into some disrepute because of their extreme dependence upon the logical relations observed to the disregard of facts of geographical distribution and culture history. As soon as it appeared that the logical sequence as determined by the analysis of the process in question was not consistent with the geographical and other facts, confidence was lost in the method and a reaction set in toward the other extreme. The result is that for some years anthropologists have ignored the whole problem of the genetic or historical development of man's material culture. The problem is, of course, none the less real for that.

The following investigation was undertaken in the anthropological laboratory of the Museum with the view of raising anew the question as to the validity of the method of logical analysis. The subject chosen was the dress of the North American Indians of the Plains and adjacent territories. The method was to study intensively the types of dress and their structural processes in the Plains area and then to extend the study less intensively to the continent and to the world at large.

We shall base our discussion almost wholly upon two types of garment, the man's shirt and the woman's dress. The sharp contrast that now exists between the costumes of European men and women is not observable among primitive peoples, the rule is for the sexes to use the same fundamental pattern. Thus, if the men wear trousers, the women do also, although the cut may be different. It is chiefly owing to this that we can make effective use of the dress of both sexes among the Plains Indians. In passing, one may remind the reader that this difference in the degree of contrast between the costumes of men and women is not a distinguishing characteristic between primitive and civilized peoples for like most phenomena of cultures the European divergence in patterns has a definite historical explanation.

Fig. 1 (1–2721). A Nez Percé Shirt. Collected about 1865. The pattern is shown in Fig. 7a.

Fig. 2 (50.1–301).   A Dakota Shirt.   For pattern see Fig. 7*b*.

Fig. 3 (50–4277). A Gros Ventre Shirt. This is part of the regalia for the dog dance, see this series, vol. 1, 255. For pattern see Fig. 8*g*.

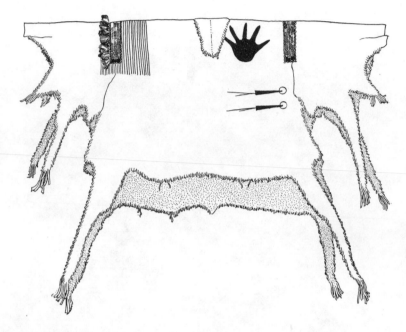

Fig. 4 (50–841).   A Man's Shirt of the Poncho Type.   This specimen is made of two-deerskins.   There are bands of quillwork over each shoulder, fringed on one side with crow feathers.   On the opposite side of the fold is a transverse band of quillwork.   See Bulletin of this Museum, vol. 18, fig. 95.   The tail tuft is discernible on the lower edge and the dewclaws are still attached to the leg projections.   Collected in 1838.

MEN'S GARMENTS.

If one take a typical man's shirt of the Plains area and suspend it, the sleeve and shoulder line will be found horizontal and to coincide. In other words there is a neck hole, but no collar (Fig. 4). If on the other hand, one suspend a true coat (Fig. 11), the familiar European sleeve and shoulder cut is seen. This may be generalized by classing the former as of the poncho type and the latter as of the coat type.

First, we may note the structure of the poncho type. Fig. 4 represents a specimen collected about 1838. There is another old specimen in the Nez Percé collection (Fig. 1). A more modern specimen is shown in Fig. 2. A simpler but old and interesting specimen is Fig. 3. From these sketches the general pattern concept is clear. Two whole skins of mountain sheep or other ruminants are taken and cut as in Fig. 5. Thus, the peculiar contour of sleeve extensions, or capes, is explained as also that of the skirt (Fig. 6). The whole pattern of this type of shirt is seen to be correlated with the contour of the natural material, and it seems most probable that it was this form of the material that suggested the pattern.

The former distribution of this type of shirt cannot be precisely stated, but so far we have found it to prevail among the Dakota, Nez Percé, Gros Ventre, Blackfoot, Crow, Hidatsa-Mandan, Pawnee,[1] Assiniboin, Arapaho, Ute, Comanche, Kiowa, and Cheyenne. It occurs, but less universally among the Sarsi, Plains-Cree, and Ojibway on the north and on the south among the Apache and in the pueblo of Taos.

Our museum collection contains about forty shirts of this poncho type, all of which we have examined in detail. Among them we find many minor variations in pattern, but so far as we can see these are all adjustments to the coat type and to new materials and, hence, due to white contact. The tendency to use cow skins and cloth is very strong and in these materials the natural contour, the base of the pattern, is wanting. This is particu-

---

[1] "A jacket, made like a shirt, of beaver or otter skins, and ornamented with beads, was highly coveted, and was beyond the command of any but the privileged few. The finest article of Indian apparel I ever saw was one of these jackets made from four otter skins. The body was formed of two pelts, and each arm of one. The skin of the head, tail, feet and even the claws of all the animals were preserved intact in the garment, and the whole richly trimmed with beads. Similar garments were also made of fine cloth, fringed with swan's down, and heavily beaded." — Dunbar, The Pawnee Indians, Magazine of American History, IV, 280.

According to James R. Murie these shirts were so rare that they should be ignored, the fact being that Pawnee men did not wear upper garments of any kind, simply a robe.

larly noticeable in the cut of the bottom as shown in Figs. 7–9. In most cases this curve is simplified by dropping the tail projection in the center, observable in the older type, Fig. 7*b*, but in one Arapaho piece we find an interesting rectangular cut at the corresponding point, Fig. 7*e*.

A comparison of the tops of these sketches shows that the shoulder

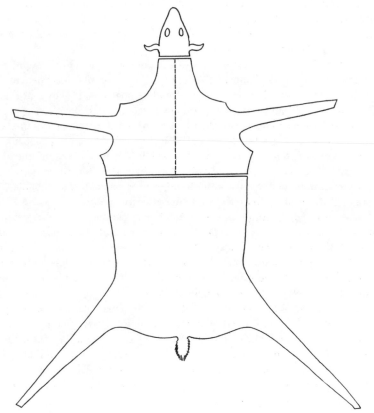

Fig. 5.   Diagram showing how a Skin is cut and folded to make a Shirt of the Poncho Type.

extensions tend to become true sleeves and the sides of the shirt are often entirely or partially sewn up in which case a vertical cut is made on the breast at the neck without which it would be next to impossible to get into the garment. The older ponchos have neither fronts nor backs, both sides being alike, but many of the modern variants have a distinct front. It is chiefly these variations in association with slight inessential modifications calling to mind features of European shirts that suggest that we have in Fig. 7a and 7b the original type of poncho for men in the Plains area.

This is further reinforced by a study of sleeve forms which in the older skin specimens follow the patterns of Figs. 7a and 7c. The sleeve pattern of Fig. 8i is found most often in cloth and distinctly modern skin pieces.

So far we have concerned ourselves with the pattern alone, but the most characteristic features of these ponchos are decorative. In all specimens of the older type these take approximately the same forms. The most conspicuous of these features are the broad beaded or quilled bands. These

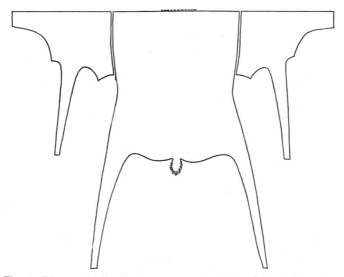

Fig. 6. Diagram showing the Arrangement of Pieces cut from the Preceding.

are made on separate strips of skin and readily detached from the shirt. From each side of the neck a band runs along the shoulder seam almost to the ends of the sleeves. At right angles to this so as to fall over the shoulders like suspenders are two other bands, one for each side. At the neck, both front and back, are triangular flaps also bearing beaded and quilled decorations. The edges of these bands are often strung with rows of feathers, strips of white weasel skins or human hair. It is due to the latter that these ponchos are often called "scalp-shirts." In the older types particularly, the edges of the body and sleeves were notched and fringed. These characteristics were almost universal but there are in addition, tribal

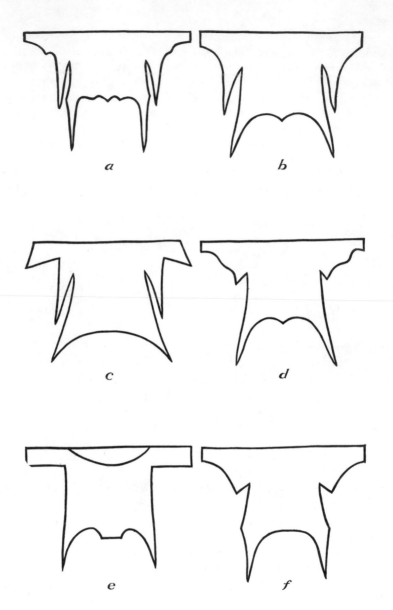

Fig. 7 (1–2721, 50.1–301, 50.1–1186, 1–2712, 50.1–37, 50.1–653).　Shirt Patterns for Men:
a Nez Percé; *b* Dakota; *c* Dakota; *d* Nez Percé; *e* Arapaho; *f* Crow.

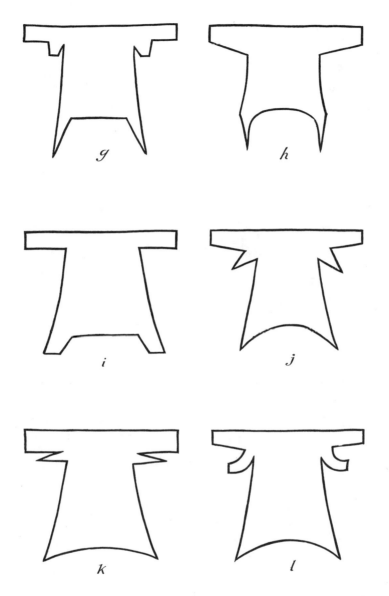

Fig. 8 (50–4277, 50–7863, 50.1–304, 50.1–761, 50.1–7370, 50.1–7212). Shirt Patterns, continued: *g* Gros Ventre; *h* Dakota; *i* Dakota; *j* Arapaho; *k* Ojibway; *l* Cheyenne?.

and regional decorations. Thus, many Blackfoot ponchos bear large circular designs on the breast and back. According to Maximilian, this was formerly common among the Assiniboin and a few other northern tribes. Dakota ponchos in particular, are frequently painted in two ground colors, bearing heraldic devices. The beaded or quilled bands have tribal peculiarities also. In another paper of this series we shall consider the probable origins of these various decorations.

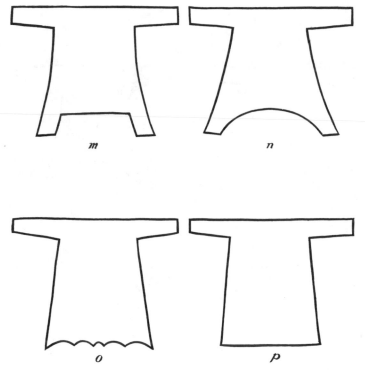

Fig. 9 (50.1–1303, 50.1–1301, 50.1–6321, 50.1–926). Shirt Patterns, concluded: *m* Apache; *n* Cheyenne; *o* Kiowa; *p* Pawnee.

Returning to the coat-like features of the more modern forms of poncho, we may be reminded that the coat form is not necessarily of European origin. The Eskimo and most Déné tribes cut a coat-like garment that fits the neck and shoulders and has sleeves, but the best known and most distinctly coat-like form is that of the Naskapi, Fig. 10. Here the pattern is most clearly cut to fit the human form as in European tailoring. With slight variations this pattern extends through the Cree to the Rocky Mountains and thence to the Salish of British Columbia. It even dips into the Plains as shown in the old Gros Ventre specimen (Fig. 12).

The garments of the western Déné area are not very well known, but in Alaska some of the modern natives wear a coat with flaring skirts like the Naskapi and certain Siberian styles. It is therefore probable that the Naskapi form is aboriginal and not due to European influence. Thus, in certain Iroquois skin coats we find a clear attempt to cut a close-fitting garment, suggesting the styles of colonial days (Fig. 13). Some other skin coats in the collection are cut in a simpler pattern, but still show the same intent. If we compare these with the Naskapi pattern the difference is clear, for here a large piece of skin is taken for the back and two for the front.[1] The flaring effect is produced by one or more triangular inserts. In many Iroquois coats there is a cut down the median plain of the back, a feature noted in the coats of many eastern Algonkin tribes and some of the Déné. On the other hand, the Naskapi mode of side seams is noted among the Sarsi, Ojibway, Menomini, Winnebago, and Penobscot. It seems therefore that the poncho form and the Naskapi coat form have their parallels among other tribes, but that in contrast to these we have a decidedly European-like cut of coat extending from the Iroquois through Canada to the Salish.

---

[1] The Naskapi winter coat is usually sewed up in front. We find that a whole skin is taken for the back piece, the tail at the bottom, and the sides trimmed to give a waist and the flaring skirt. The neck piece forms the pendant collar and the sides are pierced to give the shoulder lines. The front of the coat is of a whole skin like the back, but cut down through the middle. In the coats with sewed up fronts this is curious, because the maker cuts the skin in halves and then sews it up again.

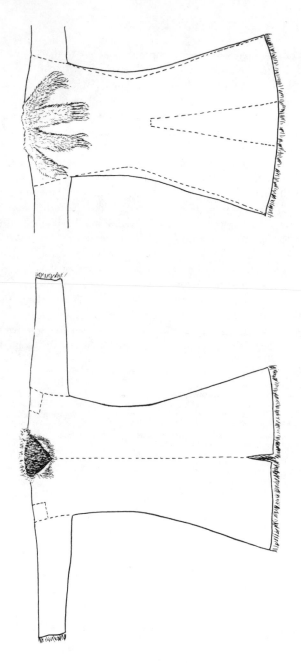

Fig. 10 (50–1721).   Pattern of a Naskapi Coat.

58

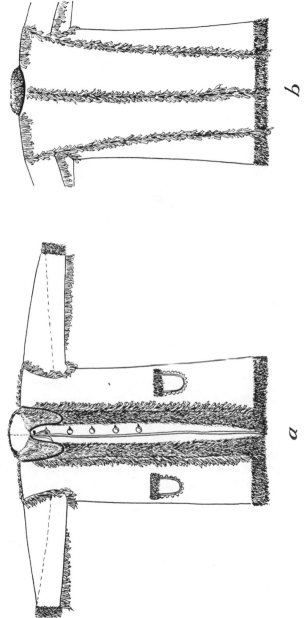

Fig. 11 (16–4576). Man's Coat of Deerskin, Thompson. In this specimen we have clearly the tailoring lines of the European Coat.

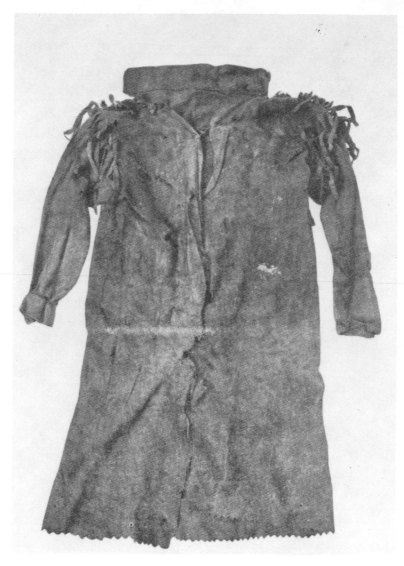

Fig. 12 (50–1924). Man's Coat, Gros Ventre. An old specimen made of dressed
buffalo skin. The pattern is simple, the body being a single piece of skin. In addition to the
attached collar the coat is composed of but three pieces.

Fig. 13 (50.1–1775).   Man's Coat of Deerskin, Onondaga.

Fig. 14 (50–6532). Man's Coat of Deerskin, Cayuga, collected by M. R. Harrington, 1907. This is a unique example of tailoring skill, for a boy's coat was split down the back, pieces inserted, and a skirt added. The beaded tomahawks were formerly the tail ornaments of the small coat. Notwithstanding its composite pattern, the lines of the body have been closely followed. Worn by William Henry Fishcarrier, a Cayuga chief. Photographed with coat, Plate LXIV, Twenty-first Annual Report, Bureau of American Ethnology.

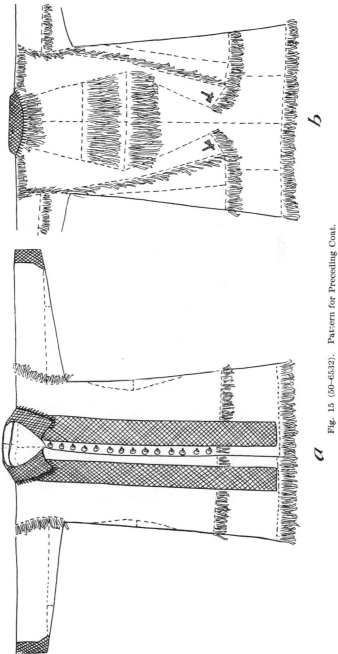

a

b

Fig. 15 (50–6532). Pattern for Preceding Coat.

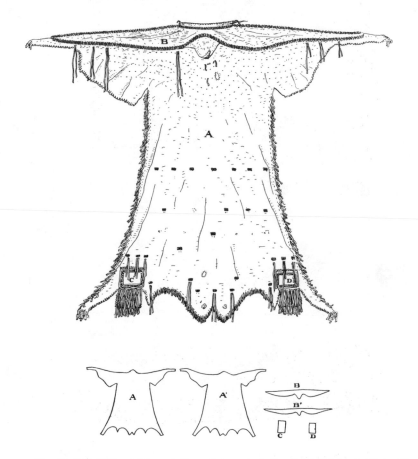

Fig. 16 (50.1–654). A Woman's Dress, Crow. An entire elkskin is taken for each side.
A cape-like yoke is formed of two pieces as above, and sewed in place. The tail projection on
b hangs loosely over a corresponding one on *a*.

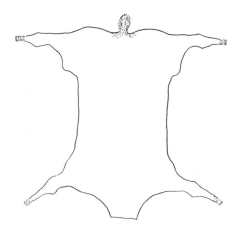

Fig. 17.   Contour of an Elkskin.   In tanning, the hair is left on the tail and the feet.
Two of these skins are required to make a dress.   See Figs. 16 and 18.

WOMEN'S GARMENTS.

The costume for women is in its fundamental technique similar to that for men.   Taking a Crow specimen as the type (Fig. 16) we see that three pieces of skin are used: an inserted yoke and two large pieces for the skirt. The sides are sewed up from the bottom of the skirt almost to the cape-like extension at the shoulders.   There are no sleeves, but the cape-like shoulder piece falls down loosely over the arms.   The side seams and the bottom and all outer edges are fringed.   The garment has neither front nor back, both sides being the same.

The technical concept is again a garment made from two whole skins, in this case, elkskins.   A dress is formed by placing two whole skins face to face, the tail ends at the top, the head at the bottom.   The neck is fitted and the yoke formed by the insertion of a transverse piece of skin.   Very little trimming is needed to shape the sides of the skirt.

The distribution of this pattern concept so far as we were able to determine by the study of specimens is: Arapaho, Assiniboin, Apache, Blackfoot, Crow, Cheyenne, Comanche, Dakota, Gros Ventre, Hidatsa, Kiowa, Nez Percé, Northern Shoshoni, Plains-Cree, Sarsi, Ute, Yakima.

We come now to the consideration of variations in the pattern.   While the fundamental form holds throughout the above distribution, there are a number of distinct cuts for the contour of the yoke and the bottom of the skirt.   Yet, there is very little variation within the tribe, it is truly surprising how precisely each of the tribes we have studied followed a definite form for the bottoms of their dresses, making it clear that they had a fixed mode, or style for the cut. This will be more fully discussed in another connection.

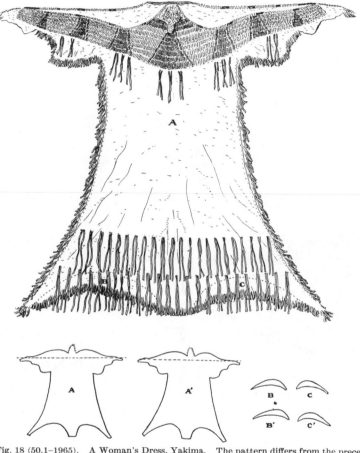

Fig. 18 (50.1–1965). A Woman's Dress, Yakima. The pattern differs from the preceding in that there is no insert at the top, merely a folding over as indicated. Separate curved pieces are inserted at the bottom to give the required contour.

European trade brought within the reach of these tribes the finest of cloth. A special quality known as strouding was always popular and from the very first was substituted for skins in making garments. This new material had a shape of its own and consequently presented a new problem to the Plains dressmaker. One example is shown in Fig. 21. A more common way was to take a rectangular piece of cloth, cut a neck hole in the middle, join the sides by triangular inserts and add shoulder extensions. In many cases the bottom of the skirt is cut out to conform to the old style. Thus it is clear that the original two skin concept was able to prevail over the introduction of new materials.

When we turn to ornamentation we find these dresses quite decorative. In contrast to men's ponchos, we find the tail of the elk falling in the center of the breast, but like them in the tendency toward horizontal decorations with quills and beads. While there is considerable tribal variation in decoration, the general tendency is to bead or quill more or less completely the entire yoke. The edges of the yoke and the skirt are usually fringed and sometimes the latter faced with a narrow band of beads. Upon the body of the skirt will be found a varying number of pendant thongs. Among the Blackfoot symbolic devices of red cloth are often found near the bottom of the skirt and similar attachments are noted on some Sarsi, Crow, and Assiniboin dresses.

HISTORICAL RELATIONS.

One general problem arising from this study is the historical relations between the several varieties of costume which in turn naturally leads to that other question as to whether structural similarities can be taken as evidence for genetic relationship. The subject may be best presented by reviewing the literature now available.

West of the Plains Area we have a large extent of territory in which no upper garment of this kind appears. The men tend toward nudity while the women wear a short skirt. The upper garment usually takes the form of a cape or is simply a robe. This is the case in California and some parts of the Shoshonean area but on the whole the Shoshonean tribes incline toward the types we have described. In the Columbia River region and northward, particularly among the Salish, we again find the poncho types of the Plains. The data furnished by Teit for the Thompson, Shuswap, and Lillooet are sufficiently detailed to permit of an analytic comparison. In the first place we find the poncho shirt for men.[1] The most distinctively poncho in type is a Thompson specimen, (16–1057, Teit, Fig. 162), made from a single piece of buffalo skin. There are no sleeves and the bottom is cut square; the sides are laced somewhat as in Plains shirts, but the neck is different. There is a circular neck hole with a vertical slit on the breast and a collar is set on the edges of the hole. This we are assured was the

---

[1] The Thompson Indians of British Columbia (Memoirs, American Museum of Natural History, vol. 2, part 4, New York, 1900).

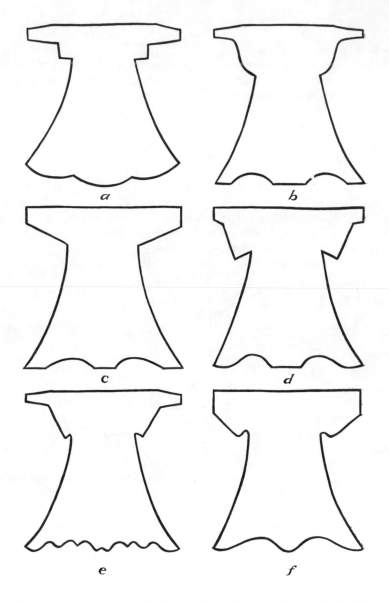

Fig. 19.　Dress Patterns: *a* Yakima; *b* Nez Percé; *c* Blackfoot; *d* Sarsi; *e* Crow; *f* Assiniboin.

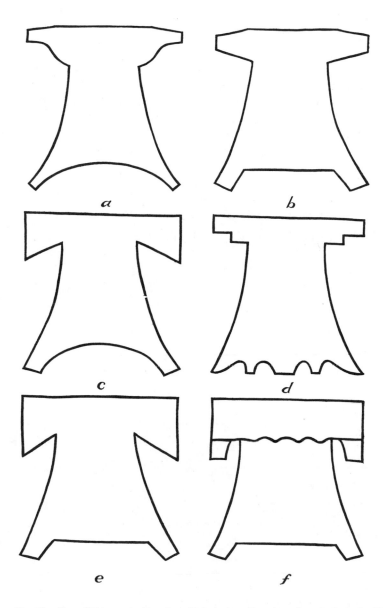

Fig. 20. Dress Patterns, continued: *a* Dakota (an alternate pattern is shown in Fig. 27); *b* Cheyenne; *c* Shoshoni; *d* Ute; *e* Arapaho; *f* Kiowa.

style for the buffalo skin shirts. On the other hand, there were buckskin shirts made of a single piece but with short sleeves (Fig. 163, Teit). In these again we have a circular neck hole but no collar. There is yet another type of man's upper garment, a true coat, previously noted. The cut of the neck is again as in the ponchos. Thus, the one distinctive feature in Thompson ponchos and coats is the cut of the neck, it being to all intents a coat cut and even in ponchos often fitted with a collar.

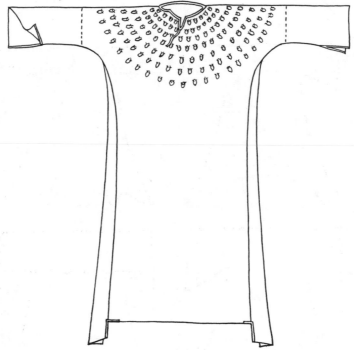

Fig. 21 (50.1–314). Dress of Blue Strouding, Brulé. Most cloth dresses in the Plains are similar in pattern. The front and back may be one piece with a hole cut for the head. The sides may be trimmed, but usually they are not. Angular pieces are inserted at the sides.

One other man's garment should be noted. The entire skin of a wolf or other animal was often worn over a poncho or coat, not so much as an extra protection as for ceremonial purposes.

The women of the Thompson wore a shirt-like dress with sleeves cut very much like the man's coat. It was open on the shoulders and laced there. The bottoms were square cut. As an under garment they wore a shirt of woven materials or a buckskin bodice.

This introduces us to another feature of Thompson clothing, the weaving of bark and hair. Garments of this material were confined to skirts and capes. Where, as among the Lillooet and Lower Thompson, they were in general use (Teit, 219), skin ponchos and coats were rare. As the weaving of bark and hair is widely distributed in this area and is practically universal among the Salish, it seems most likely that the skin poncho and the coat are due to influence from the east. We failed to find close structural parallels, however, between the Plains type and these skin garments, they being more like the coat type of the north. Yet Teit states that,

> The shirts worn by the men reached halfway to the knees, and were generally made of two doe or buck skins sewed together (necks down). The sleeves were wide, and the neck was furnished with a lacing. The hind-legs of the skin formed the sleeves; and along the entire length of the back of each was a fringe of cut skin, this being the only ornament.[1]

This is essentially the structural concept of the Plains. Again, the same writer says of the Shuswap: —

> Some women's shirts had wide sleeves and two flaps turned down from the neck which reached to the middle of the chest and back respectively. These flaps were cut in various shapes but most commonly they were square. They were fringed along the bottom, and ornamented with quills, beads, and shells.[2]

Here also we have what reads like the accounts of the Plains-Cree.[3] It also reminds one of the dress now found among the Apache in the south. All this makes it clear that the structural concept of the Plains must have been in at least partial use among the Salish, along with the coat concept. We see, however, that underlying these forms were the much more common garments of woven materials following patterns of their own.

Turning now to the east, we find another important variant among the Plains-Cree and some of the Ojibway, our data taking us back to the period of first exploration.

For the Cree we may quote from Mackenzie: —

> The coat, or body covering, falls down to the middle of the leg, and is fastened over the shoulders with cords, a flap or cape turning down about eight inches, both before and behind, and agreeably ornamented with quill-work and fringe; the bottom is also fringed, and fancifully painted as high as the knee. As it is very loose, it is enclosed round the waist with a stiff belt, decorated with tassels, and fastened behind,

---

[1] Teit, *ibid.*, 206.

[2] Teit, The Shushwap Indians (Memoirs, American Museum of Natural History, vol. 2, part 4, New York, 1909), 502.

[3] Harmon, D. W., A Journal of Voyages and Travels in the Interior of North America, New York, 1904, 275.

The arms are covered to the wrist, with detached sleeves, which are sewed as far as the bend of the arm; from thence they are drawn up to the neck, and the corners of them fall down behind, as low as the waist.[1]

Harmon[2] gives a somewhat fuller statement, but one that is curiously like that of Mackenzie: —

The shirt or coat, which is so long as to reach the middle of the leg, is tied at the neck, is fringed around the bottom, and fancifully painted, as high as the knee. Being very loose, it is girded around the waist with a stiff belt, ornamented with tassels, and fastened behind. The arms are covered as low as the wrists with sleeves, which are not connected with the body garment. These sleeves are sewed up, as far as the bend of the arm, having the seam the under side; and extend to the shoulders, becoming broader toward the upper end, so that the corners hang down as low as the waist. They are connected together, and kept on, by a cord, extending from one to the other, across the shoulders.

Again we have the statement of Henry: —

The shift or body-garment reaches down to the calf, where it is generally fringed and trimmed with quill-work; the upper part is fastened over the shoulders by strips of leather; a flap or cape hangs down about a foot before and behind, and is ornamented with quill-work and fringe. This covering is quite loose, but tied around the waist with a belt of stiff parchment, fastened on the side, where also some ornaments are suspended. The sleeves are detached from the body-garment; from the wrist to the elbow they are sewed, but thence to the shoulder they are open underneath and drawn up to the neck, where they are fastened across the breast and back. — Journal of Henry and Thompson, 514.

Grinnell[3] says of the Blackfoot: —

The ancient dress of the women was a shirt of cowskin, with long sleeves tied at the wrist, a skirt reaching half-way from knees to ankles, and leggings tied above the knees, with sometimes a supporting string running from the belt to the leggings. In more modern times, this was modified, and a woman's dress consisted of a gown or smock, reaching from the neck to below the knees. There were no sleeves, the armholes being provided with top coverings, a sort of cape or flap, which reached to the elbows. Leggings were of course still worn. They reached to the knee, and were generally made, as was the gown, of the tanned skins of elk, deer, sheep, or antelope. (196).

In early times the Assiniboin women are said to have dressed like the Cree (vol. 5, 137).

---

[1] Mackenzie, Alexander, Voyages from Montreal, on the River St. Lawrence, through the Continent of North America, to the Frozen and Pacific Oceans, in the years 1789 and 1793, etc., London, 1801, XCIV.

[2] Harmon, *ibid.*, 275.

[3] Blackfoot Lodge Tales, New York, 1903.

Fig. 22 (50.1–7369). A Cloth Dress, Plains-Ojibway, Cowesses Reserve, Saskatchewan. The front and back are the same, the garment hanging from the shoulders by the decorated straps. In this case a modern calico sleeved waist was worn as an upper garment.

Fig. 23. A Cree Dress in the Field Museum of Natural History. The material is deer-skin throughout. The skin is folded over at the top and on the shoulders there are laces. Collected in Manitoba.

For the Eastern Dakota we have the early account of Carver [1] which
is not so explicit but is supplemented by a drawing: —

Such as dress after their ancient manner, make a kind of shift with leather, which
covers the body but not the arms.   (229).

In the illustration the women's upper garment appears to be joined over
the shoulders, possibly by straps.

It is clear that all these observers are reporting upon the same general
type of costume which possesses new features as the detached cape-like
sleeves, the shoulder straps, and the turned down flaps. A specimen of
this type from the Ojibway, though somewhat modernized, will be found
in Miss Densmore's volume on Chippewa Music (II, 223). Here we find
the separate sleeves and a skirt held up at the shoulders by straps. It is
also stated that formerly a blanket was taken for the skirt and the surplus
length folded down at the breast upon which decorations were placed.[2] This
tallies very well with the remarks of Harmon and Henry and is thus readily
identified.

In 1913 Mr. Skinner observed a Plains-Ojibway (Manitoba) woman
wearing a cloth skirt of this form, Fig. 22. The shoulder straps and the
intervening flap are decorated. Instead of the detached sleeves, she wore
a simple calico waist cut like a modern shirt. It was ascertained, however,
that formerly detached sleeves were worn with these skirts. There is a
similar cloth skirt in the Museum's Penobscot collection but without the
shoulder bands or the ornamental flaps. Again at Lake St. Joseph, Mr.
Skinner collected a complete skin costume in this style, (Figs. 24–25). Here
we see the turned down flap in front and behind.

Dr. Hough informs us that in the Turner collection at the United States
National Museum there is a doll from the Nenenot dressed in this type of
costume. The Field Museum of Natural History has a dress from the
Plains-Cree which is also of this type, (Fig. 23). In this we see the detached sleeves extending over the shoulders to the neck. The dress is open
across the entire top and laced at the sides. The turned down flap noted
by early observers is here also.

It is well to note the structural peculiarity of this type, for instead of
the coat-like shirt of some Salish we have an upper garment reduced to a
pair of large sleeves extending over the shoulders to the neck and held
together only by a string, while the skirt is almost full length and held
above the breasts by shoulder straps, instead of being hung to the waist.

---

[1] Carver, John, Travels through the Interior Portions of North America in the years
1766, '67, and 68, London, 1781.
[2] Also Plate 17 in Schoolcraft, part 5.

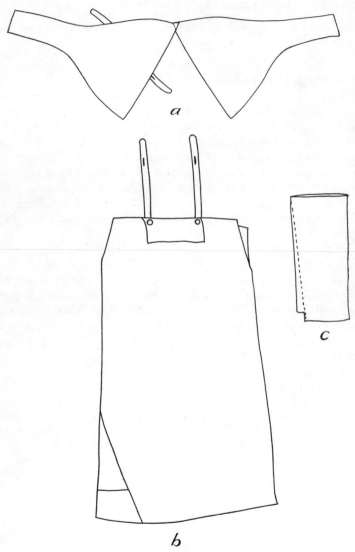

Fig. 24 (*a*, 50–8000; *b*, 50–7999, *c*, 50–8001). A Dress of Deerskin, Saulteaux, from Lake St. Joseph, Ontario. *a*, the sleeves as seen from the back; *b*, the skirt; *c*, the leggings.

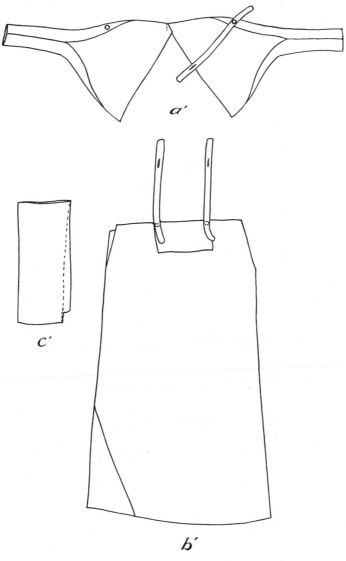

a´

c´

b´

Fig. 25. Reverse of the Preceding Garment.

Mr. Willoughby has described two old specimens credited to the Plains-Cree.[1] In these specimens we find a dress made of two rectangular pieces of skin, one piece forming the skirt and the other the waist.   The former

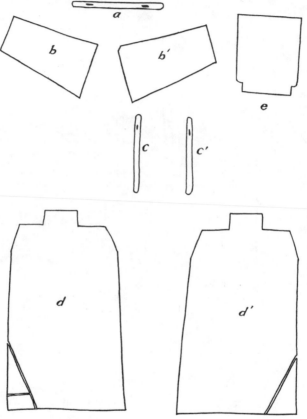

Fig. 26.   Patterns for Parts of the Dress shown in Figs. 24–25.   *a*, throat strap for holding sleeves in place; *b*, *b′* shape of piece forming sleeves; *c*, *c′* shoulder straps; *d*, *d′* pieces to form the skirt; *e*, piece for legging.

has the seam at the side and is thus very much like an Algonkin slit skirt. The waist is peculiar in that it is double.   He says: —

The piece forming the upper portion of the garment is folded horizontally through the center, then perpendicularly in the middle.   A slit is cut through the upper half of the second fold for one arm.   The upper folded edges are joined over the shoulders with a short strap and thongs, but the side for the other arm is left open.[1]

Somewhat like this was the method of wearing robes among many of the Algonkins, viz., to fasten their edges over one shoulder and leave the other arm free.[2] It seems, therefore, quite probable that in this curious folded waist to the dress we have a modified form of the robe or blanket. The probability of this is increased by the data as to sleeves. Willoughby has made very clear the general use of one or two detached muff-like sleeves among the Algonkin of the east and since the preceding quotations leave no doubt as to the use of such sleeves by the Cree at the time when these dresses were worn, one may suspect that their association has a historical basis.

Thus this extension of our quest for types has taken us into the eastern region of the skirt-like garment. It appears that everywhere in the United States east of the Mississippi, except among some Siouan and Central Algonkin tribes the women wore a skirt fastened at the waist. One form of this is often spoken of as the Algonkin slit skirt, though it was used by the Iroquois and perhaps a number of southern tribes. It even found its way into the southern Plains.

Thus Dunbar gives us a very definite statement for the Pawnee:—

The dress of the women consisted of moccasins, leggins; tightly laced above the knee, and reaching to the ankles, a skirt covering from the waist to below the knee, and a loose waist or jacket suspended from the shoulders by straps. The arms were bare, except when covered by the robe or blanket. The garments of the women, other than the moccasins, were made, if the wearer could afford it, of cloth, otherwise of some kind of skin, dressed thin and soft. — Magazine of American History, IV, p. 268.

Probably the same kind of garment was used by the Cheyenne for we read in the account of Long's Expedition that: —

Their costume is very simple, that of the female consisting of a leathern petticoat, reaching the calf of the leg, destitute of a seam, and often exposing a well-formed thigh, as the casualties of wind or position influence the artless foldings of the skirt. The leg and foot are often naked, but usually invested by gaiters and mockasins. A kind of sleeveless short gown, composed of a single piece of the same material, loosely clothes the body, hanging upon the shoulders, readily thrown off, without any sense of indelicacy, when suckling their children, or under the influence of a heated atmosphere, displaying loose and pendant mammæ. A few are covered by the more costly attire of coarse red or blue cloth, ornamented with a profusion of blue and white beads: the short gown of this dress has the addition of wide sleeves

---

[1] American Anthropologist, vol. 7, N. S., 640
[2] *Ibid.*, 504.

descending below the elbow; its body is of a square form, with a transverse slit in the upper edge for the head to pass through; around this aperture, and on the upper side of the sleeves, is a continuous stripe, the breadth of the hand, of blue and white beads, tastefully arranged in contrast with each other, and adding considerable weight as well as ornament to this part of the dress. Around the petticoat, and in a line with the knees, is an even row of oblong conic bells, made of sheet copper, each about an inch and a half in length, suspended vertically by short leathern thongs as near to each other as possible, so that when the person is in motion, they strike upon each other, and produce a tinkling sound.[1]

Mr. A. C. Parker of the State Museum in Albany supplies the following information as to Iroquois costume: —

I have found that these early Indian women did wear a tunic or over dress made of two deerskins fastened into a sort of sleeveless gown. The necks of the pelts were trimmed off in most cases and holes were made in the side of the skin through which cords of buckskin were drawn to fasten it together. This was done by two methods, either through large holes into which the buckskin was run as a tape or run through smaller holes placed in pairs which were tied together in short strings that hung down in front. These garments were not always fringed at the side, although I am told that they were mostly so. There was a short poncho that was made by folding a single skin in the middle and cutting a hole for the neck. This garment was often so short that it did not reach the waist. It was never fastened by a belt, so that the skin of the body was often visible under the flapping garment. The Algonkin slit skirt was an Iroquois garment in the sense that the women once wore it. I am told that in early times this garment was made by simply folding the skin about the body and tying a broad band of buckskin at the waist. The skin was folded down over this band, securing it effectually. The older garments were not sewed at the side; the slit was generally over the left leg which permitted the limb to be bared and used as a sort of work board upon which buckskin strings were rolled between it and the hand. Hemp strings were also twisted in this way, that is to say, rolled into shape. In later times when broadcloth came into use, garments of that material were patterned after the old buckskin skirt, although usually the cloth garment was sewed up the side. In most cases, however, there was a short strip reaching part way to the knee on the right side, left either partly open or simply basted together.

As to the dress patterns, my inquiries have shown that the necks of skins formed the bottom of the dress and never the top. I was told that sometimes the men used the tails at the neck but that the women did not.[2] The long pieces formed by the fore legs and neck were usually drawn to the side and slashed in the fringe, but most of the neck was entirely trimmed off. The reason apparently being that the leather was too thick and so easily stiffened that it was not an ornament. One of my informants, said that the fringe formed by the fore legs was regarded as an attractive part of the ornamentation, since it hung down at the side longer than the rest and lay upon

---

[1] Long's Expedition, 1823, vol. 3, p. 47.

[2] It is curious how widespread was the use of the tail as an ornament. Willoughby quotes Levett to the effect that in New England deerskin mantles were valued more if bearing a perfect tail (*Ibid.*, 504). They occur in Naskapi coats and then generally westward down through the Plains.

the skirt below. For this reason the front of the dress sometimes presented a "U" shaped outline, that is to say, the cut was so made that it was in a semicircular shape from one side to the other.

Of the women of New England we read: —

The women's robes were longer and fuller than those of the men. Instead of one deer or bear skin two were sewed at full length. These garments were so long as to drag on the ground 'like a great ladies train.' — Willoughby, American Anthropologist, vol. 7, 505.

Before taking up the interesting points raised by these new data we may give a moment's consideration to the slit skirt. The drawings of John White, presumably of Virginia Indians in 1585 show women wearing two aprons one before and one behind, showing as they hang a slit on either side. While this is not strictly speaking a slit skirt, the sketches give one much the same appearance. The skirt is, however, a single piece of skin and most likely an entire deerskin. The conventional cloth skirts as worn by modern Indian women have one peculiarity, a trailing strip at the slit. Now, if a deerskin were taken and drawn around the body in the natural way to form such a skirt, the neck and tail pieces would come together at the side and the skin of one fore and one hind leg would hang down the side of the leg. This would give us the same effect as is obtained in the cloth skirt by the pendant strip. While this is as yet no definite proof that this is the history of the slit skirt, it must be given great probability since we find the forms of Plains garments due to similar conditions.

To return to our consideration of upper garments we find an interesting distribution for the detached sleeve. Thus, while the Iroquois women wore a poncho-like upper garment, it had no sleeves and was quite like an abbreviated Plains dress. The idea of sleeves as a separate and distinct garment thus extends over the Eastern Woodlands and into the Plains, with the possible exception of the Iroquois.

If we take the continent as a whole, we find a great sleeveless area, comprising the greater part of the Southeastern states, the Southwest, California, and the North Pacific Coast. In the north, we have the Eskimo, Déné, and Northern Algonkin areas universally using the true sleeve. Then in the intermediate territory as among the Salish, the Plains, and Eastern Woodlands, a mixed area. Among practically all of the Eastern Woodland tribes within the United States a toga-like upper garment was worn with a single sleeve for the exposed arm. This was fastened by a string so as to be readily taken off in case of need. In the Ojibway and Western Cree country the toga-like garment disappears and two sleeves are used, but still hung by a string so that the arms can be freed at will. In pattern, these sleeves were closed only from the waist to the elbow. Now in the Plains, particularly in the north in proximity to the Cree, we find some of the sleeves for women's dresses formed by closing up the edge of the cape from elbow to wrist. We also find in the inverted yoke of the Nez Percé, etc., a piece of skin not unlike that necessary for such sleeves. In men's shirts we have also noted the same tendency toward closed sleeves and structurally the older form of sleeve (p. 52) is not unlike that used by Ojibway women. Hence, this distribution suggests that the belt of mixed sleeve types is due to opposing influences from the sleeveless and sleeved areas respectively.

This brings us to an important phase of the problem; viz., in how far can such data take us in historical interpretation? After having cited the mere facts of distribution as above can we safely say that the peculiar intermediate forms of sleeve are intrusive adjustments and as such represent diffused traits from the north?

The first thing that suggests itself is to examine the structural concepts to see how much they may have in common. If we turn to the Atlantic Coast we find a people wearing a robe for an upper garment which is fastened over the left shoulder, leaving the right arm unprotected. This impresses one as a type of costume ill-adapted to the winter climate of the latitude of New York and raises the suspicion that it was devised by a people living farther south. Further, we see an attempt to adapt it to the climate by the addition of a single sleeve for the right arm. This may well be regarded as a specific invention and not necessarily suggested by the coat-like garments of the north. In fact, one must suspect that contact with coat-wearing people would lead to the adoption of the coat *in toto*, as we find the Indian did later from the colonists. The idea of an arm covering could readily have come from a legging, or even less specific sources, simply the idea of wrapping up in something. This is, of course, speculative, but it is well to note the seeming greater probability that we have here a specific invention and not a case of incomplete borrowing. Elsewhere we have shown that the tendency in material culture seems to be the taking over of trait complexes as wholes and not in isolated fragments[1] by which the probability of this being an independent invention is heightened.

If now we take up the Ojibway sleeve we find it on a costume of a different kind. The concept here is not a skirt hung from the waist but a longer one suspended from the shoulders so as to cover the breasts. In such a garment both arms as well as the shoulders are equally exposed. In this case a coat would seem the most natural solution. We are, of course,

---

[1] American Anthropologist, vol. 16, 491.

dealing with the women's clothing for Ojibway men wore a sleeved shirt. Yet, the women sometimes used the eastern slit skirt with a sleeved jacket. Hence, that the Ojibway women did not exclusively use a sleeved jacket when such could not have been unknown to them, makes it clear that some other factors are involved. In the foregoing type we have again the concept of a sleeve fastened to the neck by a string, encasing the fore arm but hanging loosely over the upper arm and the shoulder. So far as we have data there are no essential differences from the sleeve of the Eastern Algonkin. The important point here is, that a pair is used instead of one. The reason for this, appearing that this body costume leaves both arms exposed. Since the Ojibway through their various divisions were at one time in touch with the main body of Algonkin tribes and have several material traits in common, it is fair to assume that the detached sleeves of both had a common origin. On purely logical grounds, one must suspect that the Ojibway were acquainted with the single sleeve costume before they took to a pair, but this may be far from the truth.

The next case in which technological descent is suggested is the cape and sleeves found in certain Plains dresses. Thus, if we took an Ojibway costume and sewed the shoulder extensions of the sleeves to the front and back of the skirt we should have essentially the same garment as found among the Nez Percé and some neighboring tribes. In fact the structural agreement is so close that a historical relationship can scarcely be denied. Thus, in the skirt as described by Harmon, Henry, Teit, et. al., the two skins from which it was made were folded down at the top and the decoration made upon the pendant flap, and in some of the Plains dresses we find a similar folding over before the material is sewed down to the neck piece. Again, the shape of the inserted neck piece or yoke is about the same as the piece one would cut for the Ojibway sleeve. It may also be noted that the decorations of Plains dresses are in every case on the part of the dress corresponding to the pendant flap of the Ojibway type. Hence, it is difficult to conceive of independent steps that would lead to these correspondences.

Though the origin of the Plains woman's skirt is somewhat obscure, it seems to be a structural concept of two entire skins joined in a definite manner, the tails at the top, the necks at the bottom. Since the skirt covers the entire person and hangs from the shoulders without sleeves, one must again suspect that a genetic relation exists between this dress and the Ojibway type although it is not so convincing as the case of the sleeves because the fundamental structural concept is merely the use of two skins. While this concept is clear in the Plains, it appears among the Salish and again among the Iroquois in less definite pattern associations. Against its acceptance may be offered the supposition that the adjustment is nothing but a natural process of economizing in material, and that since the form of a skin was everywhere the same such methods would result as a matter of course. On the other hand, if we look at North American costume as a whole we may see that tailoring, or cutting of materials to fit the body has but a limited distribution. It is among the Eskimo that tailoring reaches a high standard, the patterns seemingly adjusted to the lines of the body and the demands of decoration without regard to the natural contour of the material. Even among the Déné peoples the tendency is marked as shown in certain sketches by Dr. Hatt.[1] In all these garments we find a cut so devised as to fit the coat to the neck and shoulders. Of this the man's and woman's garment of the Plains is innocent, the top of the garment being straight. It is also quite noticeable that certain Salish woman's costumes have this straight cut and even Naskapi coats approach it. On the other hand, as we have noted, some Salish and Iroquois coats show tailoring and shoulder fitting.

Now it appears that the two-skin garment is not conceived upon tailoring lines but rather upon draping the figure, or hanging a covering over it. The tendency to make the most of the natural material is thus after all a part of the process and if it does occur in different localities, we find it as part of a concept complex in which the idea of tailoring is not found. We may, therefore, assume that the two-skin method indicates the presence of an unfitted body covering, usually without attached sleeves. The center of distribution for this type seems to have been the Plains.

Now let us see to what this discussion has brought us. In reviewing the data we had reason to doubt historical connections between the detached sleeves and coat garments farther north, but on the other hand, there was good ground for assuming a historical connection between the sleeves of the Ojibway type and those found upon women's dresses, among the Nez Percé and vicinity. Again, the use of two skins as a structural concept appears to be independent of the tailoring methods of the north and to center in the Plains.

We are sometimes puzzled because, while the point of view in modern ethnology professes to be historical, we often find no historical data available. Thus we may be challenged to show how one can form any safe conclusion as to the origin of these types of costume in the absence of historic data. The place of the latter is often taken by archaeological data, but in this case there are none. Yet, there are some historical data. The Blackfoot, for example, claim to have taken to the sleeveless Plains type

---

[1] Hatt, Gudmund, Arktiske Skïnddragter i Eurasien og Amerika, København, 1914.

of woman's dress recently; the Cheyenne were observed in 1820 vacillating between two forms of costume and later going over entirely to the Plains type. Among the Salish the chronology of the types is not clear, but we infer that the Plains type was used so long ago that it does not appear in Museum collections. Since the time of Carver the Eastern Dakota seem to have shifted from the Ojibway type to that of the Plains. The Assiniboin are first credited with the Ojibway type. This rather clearly restricts the origin of the Plains type to the Nez Percé, Crow, Mandan, Hidatsa, Arapaho, Kiowa, and some of the Shoshoni and since these form a contiguous geographical group, the trait is as closely localized as we can expect.

In precisely the same manner we may treat the data for the shirt. Our collections show that the older specimens are of the characteristic type (Fig. 7a) and that the newer pieces tend toward coat styles. Then we have historical data restricting this shirt formerly to a triangular area comprising little more than Idaho, Montana, and Wyoming in the United States but a much more extensive area in Canada.

It may then be asked if we have not arrived at a historical conclusion by direct means and if this is not a conclusion beyond the range of a comparative distribution of specimens? The answer to this has been given above, when we reached essentially the same result by a comparative study of specimens alone. Yet, the value of historical data is very great and the moral of the case is that such data are usually to be had for the seeking. Ethnological data are based upon direct observation or testimony and so are historic. Archaeological data are quite different for they introduce relative chronology as interpreted from physical conditions.

Now that we have some of the complexities of this problem in hand, we may try to summarize the arguments. In the first place, we have established one so-called genetic fact in that whoever devised the types of dress in the Plains arrived at the particular style from the concept of a two-skin garment; and that the style was in the beginning accidental, but once established survived the abandonment of the two-skin idea. It should be noted that this is quite another matter from accounting for the origin of costume as such, for though there is a strong probability that the two-skin idea centers in the Plains, it would be absurd to assume that it grew out of an original discovery of dress in the same locality. Taking our archaeological knowledge of North America as it stands, we may be sure that the first inhabitants of the Plains had well developed costume complexes. Hence, the only reasonable hypothesis we can form is that the two-skin garment arose when someone set about making economical use of deerskins. We have noted how the poncho idea seems to precede the two-skin and how an effort was made to add sleeves to a true poncho. Our interpretation is therefore, that if any original idea arose in the Plains it was the two-skin concept, but that if so, the inventor simply used it to create a garment that combined the ideas of a poncho and a coat. The analysis of the geographical distribution shows that along the Rocky Mountains in the region traversed by Shoshonean and Shahaptian peoples, this type of garment arose. It was not universal since many groups used extensively garments of another type made from woven materials. To the south stretching over parts of two continents was the great textile area where ponchos and sleeveless garments were the mode. To the north were the Déné and Northern Algonkin tribes fringing the Eskimo, the great area of tailored skin coats. The most probable thing is therefore that the poncho of the south was first introduced to the Shoshoni, Shahaptian, and Salish as a part of their textile development, but they were a hunting people in contact with a great area of skin coat wearers and so necessitated an adjustment. The compromises they made have been outlined in the previous discussion.

All questions of trait origins should remind us of an important problem, the actual content of a tribe's (social group unit) individuality, or the integrity of its culture. Suppose we take the woman's dress and see in how far, if at all, each of the tribes has individuality. If we take the pattern outline of dresses we note certain differences but relatively little variation within the tribe. A glance at the map (Fig. 27) will show how these are distributed. The two distinctive parts are the bottoms of the skirts and the shoulder extensions. Yet even in this respect a tribe can scarcely claim individuality for the Sarsi, Blackfoot, Assiniboin, and Nez Percé are the same. Again we find the Cheyenne, Arapaho, and Kiowa quite identical. The Dakota and Shoshoni form another group. The Hidatsa, Crow, Ute, and Apache have something in common also. The important point, however, is that these have a geographical grouping rather than a random one, thus precluding the idea of a chance agreement.

In shoulder forms there is a little more variation within the tribe and some more individuality. Thus in Fig. 28 are all the forms we found and a list of the tribes using them. The prevailing forms are shown in Fig. 27. The Dakota have two patterns but one of these is suspiciously like the man's shirt, while the other is almost identical with the Cheyenne cut. In the case of the Blackfoot, Assiniboin, and Hidatsa on one side and the Arapaho, Shoshoni, Kiowa, and Apache on the other, we have again geographical grouping.

If we take the patterns for cloth dresses, or those made of heavy strouding, we find precise uniformity throughout. The cut is plain and rectangular, Fig. 21.

It is thus clear that exact tribal individuality will be limited to very trivial and inessential features of the pattern and often lost in the range of inter-tribal variation.

The man's shirt presents greater variation, but again we find the bottom

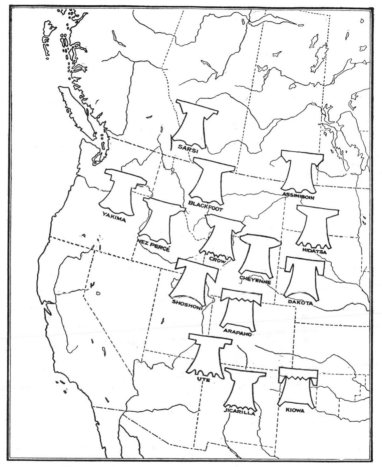

Fig. 27.   Distribution of the Plains Type of Woman's Dress.

of the garment distinctive, the several types and their distribution being given in Figs. 7–9. It should be noted, however, that the specimens following patterns of Figs. 7a and b are the oldest in the collection and that the many and widely distributed coat-like patterns of Fig. 9 are dis-

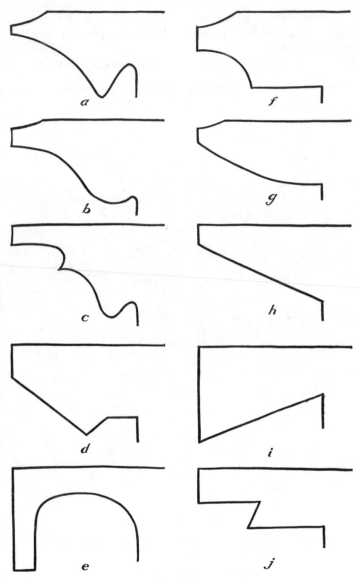

Fig. 28. Cape Patterns for Women. These are schematic and not accurately drawn from particular specimens as in Figs. 19 and 20. The observed distributions are as follows: — a Crow; b Jicarilla Apache, Nez Percé, and Yakima; c Taos; d Assiniboin and Sarsi; e and f Dakota; g Cheyenne; h Assiniboin, Blackfoot, and Hidatsa; i Arapaho, Apache, Kiowa and Shoshoni; j Ute.

tinctly recent.   Yet, making due allowance for this disturbing factor there still appears a tendency toward geographical grouping in variations of the older patterns while the others seem to be almost universally distributed.

The sleeves of shirts are somewhat analogous.   The older specimens follow the forms of Figs. 7a and b while the newer ones tend to the simple parallelogram cut of Fig. 9 which is found among all tribes.

Thus we find that none of these details in pattern or cut can be exclusively assigned to a single tribal group but are found more or less continuously distributed.   This distribution is much more restricted than that of the fundamental pattern which we have shown to prevail in the Plains, but still indicates considerable diffusion.   Should one be minute enough and possess a sufficient number of examples it would be possible to isolate further individualities but these seem to be little more than the personal equations of the individual cutters.   A generalized view would be that the fundamental pattern is widely diffused and the secondary features less so.   We have seen how the Plains type inter-relates to the Ojibway type, etc., which indicates that we are dealing with a true complex in which the more fundamental the idea the wider the distribution.

Investigations of this character are revealing what may prove to be an important general method in the study of culture.   We have in the course of this discussion developed the specific fact that centered in the Plains we find a mixed type of costume which upon analysis presents fundamental elements prevailing in two great contiguous areas.   Were this the only case of the kind it would have nothing more than a specific significance but a similar condition is found in some other traits noted in the writer's discussion of material culture.[1]   In the concluding sections to Volume XI of this series, the same condition is found with respect to certain shamanistic concepts and societies; hence, it is not merely a characteristic of material culture but one of general application.   We have shown in the preceding and the discussion of societies just cited, that recognizing this as a point of departure we can by analytic comparisons arrive at fairly satisfactory conclusions as to the historical and chronological relations of the traits involved. It seems therefore that when we find a trait complex showing intermediate forms and associations between the complexes of two geographically opposite areas, we may safely assume that its origin is due to the assimilation of borrowed concepts.

---

[1] American Anthropologist, vol. 16.

SUMMARY.

Some of the points of general significance developed in the preceding discussion may be formulated as follows: —

1. We have satisfactory proof that the characteristic style of garments for both men and women in the Plains area, was suggested by the natural contour of the materials used, or rather resulted from an economic use of the same. It is also shown how quickly the features determined by the shape of the original materials disappeared when trade cloth came into use, though the fundamental pattern remains the same, indicating that this pattern or general concept was one of structure rather than of adapted material. This leads one to suspect that the pattern concept came first to a skin-using people from some external source, most likely from the textile ponchos of the south.

2. The concept of tailoring, or cutting a garment to follow the lines of the shoulder and trunk is found in America only among the coat-wearing tribes: viz., the Eskimo, a few northern Algonkin, and the Déné, with minor representation among the Iroquois and interior Salish. Our data show how the idea tends to spread by increasing contact with Europeans. In the Old World tailoring appears again among the more primitive peoples of the north, but in historic peoples first among the Chinese. Its appearance in Western Europe is relatively recent. The idea of tailoring cloth seems not to have been developed by people anywhere except in Central Asia. It seems probable that the extensive use of the toga-like garment and the rectangular poncho, especially the latter, was due to the limitations of the weaving process and that here again the unavoidable rectangular contour of textiles is responsible for the fundamental similarities of styles. The Chinese on the other hand, escaped from these limitations by the development of tailoring. This presents another important problem: viz., did some of the northern tribes invent tailoring out of the necessity of the case or borrow it from some more highly cultured people in Central Asia? One may suspect that the Chinese were the borrowers, but in the absence of investigation this should be given little weight. In any case in the New World we find these two contrasting types of garment structure, tailoring prevailing in the far north and the opposite in the remainder of the continent, including the area of specialized textiles.

3. In respect to the area covered by the detailed comparisons in the preceding, it is clear that scarcely a single important feature of a given garment is peculiar to a single tribe but that two or more in geographical continuity share it equally. It also appears that the more fundamental a

given feature, the wider its distribution.   In other words, a tribe's individuality is merged into the mere personal variations of individual workers, and so far as these specific traits go, the limits of the social group have no significance.   Perhaps after all it is only in traits of culture where several individuals must actively cooperate, as in ritualistic performance, that the social unit is of consequence; or, unless the social unit as such functions in a trait in contrast to individuals, may we expect the bounds of the social unit to correspond with the bounds of the trait in question.

4.   The preceding data may also serve as an approach to a question of validity in evidence.   Thus, we may ask in how far mere comparative studies in the forms and distributions of traits can give light upon the historical associations of traits?   The suggestion in this case is that if the search is pushed far enough, the necessary data for a satisfactory conclusion may be found.   For perishable objects, such as costume, real historic data is usually obtainable; for the more durable, as stone, ceramics, etc., archaeological methods give a definite relative chronology.   Another important problem is as to the determination of genetic relationships in technological processes by a logical analysis of the concepts involved.   Within the limits of this study this is little more than a restatement of the above historical problem since the specific point is as to which of these types of dress, or parts of dress, as sleeves, yoke, etc., suggested or developed into the other; but when extended to the clothing of the continent or the world, tends more and more to be purely a problem of genetic relationship.   The scope of the preceding investigation is too limited to give a concrete example of this problem, and while it suggests the great difficulty of arriving at the truth without the aid of supplementary historical data, it does suggest that the future may see developed a few principles of culture diffusion which taken with the analysis of technological concepts will lead to safe conclusion as to their genesis.

5.   Finally we have found in this material trait a good case of culture diffusion.   That the secondary features such as cut of skirt-bottoms, sleeves, etc., when found to be the same for two or more tribes are so because of tribal independence in invention, is scarcely admissible because of the observed geographical continuity.   A random repetition of specific inventions should also have a random distribution to be consistent with the laws of accident.   Likewise the fundamental structural concept which underlies these secondary concepts while very widely distributed is also continuous, whence it follows that the diffusion hypothesis is the most acceptable.   We do find one disconnected locality for the two-skin concept among the Iroquois; but since these people were great travelers and had other costume concepts in general use, we may hesitate to credit them with its independent invention.

ANTHROPOLOGICAL PAPERS

OF

THE AMERICAN MUSEUM
OF NATURAL HISTORY

Vol. XVII, Part III

—

STRUCTURAL BASIS TO THE DECORATION OF COSTUMES
AMONG THE PLAINS INDIANS.

BY

CLARK WISSLER

NEW YORK
PUBLISHED BY ORDER OF THE TRUSTEES
1916

STRUCTURAL BASIS TO THE DECORATION OF COSTUMES AMONG THE PLAINS INDIANS.

By Clark Wissler.

PREFACE.

The following is a continuation of the preceding study of structural concepts in the costumes of the Plains Indians, attention here being directed to styles of ornamentation. The examples noted were first presented in the January Anthropological Lectures at this Museum in 1915. The illustrations and citations are for the most part to preceding papers in this series. Students of primitive art have often believed it possible to discover the successive steps in the evolution of designs. By arranging examples found upon prehistoric or later objects in order of their increasing conventionality, series have resulted, showing a clearly realistic drawing at one end and an almost entirely geometrical one at the other. Such series suggest that all these forms were initiated by first drawing from real life and then by successive conventionalizations arriving at a pure geometric form. The weak point in this interpretation is that there are no means of dating the units of the series, their arrangement being merely a matter of selection on the part of the observer. There are still other obvious objections to the interpretation, so that the tendency of the critical is to reject the conclusions. Somewhat analogous attempts have been made in the study of industrial arts and technology, but with equally unconvincing results. Consequently, as the case stands today, we can point to scarcely a single example in which the life history of a trait can be satisfactorily demonstrated in objective data.

In the following we have some less elaborate series of another kind but still good examples of the genesis of specific decorative designs. With one possible exception, they differ from the previous genetic studies of design in that the origin was not strictly in attempts at realistic art but merely grew out of attempts to embellish surfaces of fixed contour and to conceal unsightly lines. The exception referred to is the deer tail design upon certain Teton specimens, where we have a good case of a design arrived at, in part, by conventionalized representation.

March, 1916.

CONTENTS.

ILLUSTRATIONS.

TEXT FIGURES.

Introduction.

In the preceding paper we have analyzed the structure of certain garments found among the Plains tribes. One of the most unique points developed was the stylistic influence of the natural contours in the materials. If we push our view beyond the boundaries of the Plains, we find evidences of a like relation even in textiles, from which it appears that we have here a principle of style development. In the course of this investigation we noted somewhat analogous relations between structure and ornamentation, the subject of this discussion.

Women's Costume.

The Yakima dress (p. 66) seems to be a good example of the fundamental structure in Plains dresses. The shoulder line is here produced by the simple expedient of folding over the tail end of an elkskin. The contour of this piece is, no doubt, trimmed to a symmetrical form but still follows the lines of the original pelt. This folded over portion thus defines a peculiar curve whose origin is in the original material and not in the aesthetic constructive activities of the maker. It is, of course, true that the latter is chiefly responsible for its balance and symmetry, but the general direction of the curve was an external affair.

The chief decorations upon these dresses are the beaded yokes. In the Yakima dress we note a band along the shoulder seam where the folds of the front and back halves of the garment are sewed together, but the most prominent feature is the very broad band of beads following the curve of the turned over section. When dressing a skin for a dress the hair is left upon the tail and this tuft of hair becomes the conspicuous center piece of our broad beaded band.

Turning to the Crow dress on p. 64, we note a slightly different structure, for instead of a fold, a yoke is cut of two pieces and laid over the large skins forming the two halves of the dress. But the tail tuft and the same curve as before, mark the contour of this yoke which overlaps the garment precisely like the fold in the Yakima type. The beading of this Crow piece is far less elaborate than for the preceding but again follows the same con-

99

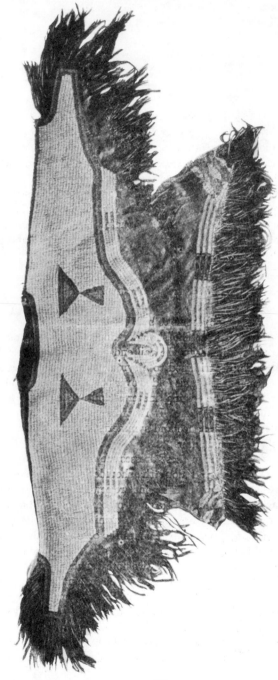

Fig. 1 (50–2021). Decoration upon a Woman's Costume. Dakota. For variants of this design see Bulletin of this Museum, vol. 18.

tour lines.   However, on the Blackfoot dress shown in vol. 5, p. 126, we have broad bands as in the Yakima case and a separate yoke like that of the Crow.

So far as our observation goes, the tail tuft is a leading feature in the group of tribes of which the Blackfoot and Crow form the center.   Further south, we find the whole upper part of the dress beaded.   Our most interesting examples are the older specimens from the Dakota of which Fig. 1 is typical.   In structure, we have a large yoke to which the skirt is attached by a straight seam.   Yet, the beading is so laid out as to give us the contour notes in the preceding and then below this and parallel to it is a broad band. There is no tail tuft but a beaded design of the same form around which the band passes with a sharp curve.   As there are a number of dresses in our Dakota collection bearing similar designs, this case is typical.   The historical relation between this decoration and those we have just discussed is obvious.

In the southern Plains we have a somewhat different dress style (p. 87). The Kiowa, Arapaho, and to some extent, the Apache, make a large rectangular yoke to which the dress is attached, but usually underneath so that we have the appearance of the folded over yoke.   On a few of these yokes we find the tail tuft, which carries us directly to the fundamental structural type.   The beaded decorations, however, do not follow the characteristic curve of the north, but the rectangular outline of this yoke.   That the curve idea was once entertained is suggested by two old specimens in the Museum bearing the tail tuft and also approximating the curved contours we have noted.[1]

If now we turn to the northern frontier of the Plains and to the Woodlands we find a similar relation between decorations and patterns.   The type for the Cree described by early writers and represented by Fig. 23, p. 74, bore decorations on the folded over yoke.   Quill designs were often placed here (p. 71).   In the modern Ojibway type (p. 73) we have the fold but the decoration is applied to the shoulder straps and to an intervening section of the yoke.

As we have shown in the preceding paper, the one connecting link between these dresses and those of the Plains is this folded over yoke.   The use of sleeves in the east and a different method of fitting the skins did not, however, give the peculiar curve we have noted in the northern Plains.   On the other hand, the dress of the southern Plains has certain analogies to the

---

[1] One of these specimens is credited to Taos and the other to the Apache and both are of primitive structure, like Fig. 18, p. 66.· The tail end of the skin is folded over and hangs down.   The decoration is chiefly a row of pendants.

Woodland type, whether due to convergence or diffusion we are unable to decide.[1]

Along with the concept of a folded over yoke goes the idea that it was the place for the most elaborate decoration. As we have previously stated, the fact that we have a continuous distribution for this association between structure and decoration, justifies the assumption of a single origin. The point here, however, is that when the structure of the yoke is modified, its style of decoration tends to change, but is not exactly correlated because in some instances the style has survived in spite of these changes.

The most interesting survival is found on Dakota dresses where, as we have stated, the tail has given way to a U-shaped conventional design. In a previous study the symbolic association with this design has been discussed.[2] Curiously enough, the design is not called a deer tail but is said to represent a turtle emerging from a lake. In the above citations, it is shown how this conforms to a mystical conception of an association between turtles and women.

If now we recall the basic facts in aboriginal decorative art, we see here a very important concrete case in which the symbolic interpretation can make no good claim to being the creative motive of the design. On the other hand, there is the very best of evidence that the design arose from the structure and the use of the homely deer tail as an ornament. The symbolic association is, therefore, secondary.

MEN'S SHIRTS.

The decorations upon shirts of the Plains men present a more perplexing problem. Reference to the illustrations in the preceding paper indicates one common conventional style. This consists in the main of a broad band over the shoulder and sleeve seam and two transverse bands like suspenders or shoulder straps. These bands are beaded or quilled strips of skin, sewed in place upon the shirt and are scarcely distinguishable from legging bands. To one edge of the bands a fringe of hair or ermine tails is attached. The oldest shirt we have seen is that shown on p. 50. The band on the top of the

---

[1] It will be noted that the yoke of the Arapaho and Kiowa is cut of a single piece. The shapes of some of these suggest that a small skin was placed transversely and a hole cut for the neck. This would give us the characteristic contour. The fold effect is secured by fastening the skirt up under the edge of the yoke. It should be considered that it is only an elkskin that is large enough for a woman's dress and that if antelope or other deer are used, piecing must be resorted to.

[2] Bulletin, American Museum of Natural History, vol. 18, p. 240; also Museum Journal, 1912.

sleeve and shoulder is upon the other side, as drawn. (See Bulletin of this Museum, vol. 18, fig. 95.) When we examine the specimen it appears that the bands cover seams. The top seam is covered by the long band and the transverse seam by the shoulder strap. However, this old shirt differs from others in that the shoulder bands are short. Further, the long shoulder bands on later shirts do not cover the seams but slant inward. This slant and greater length of the bands on newer shirts at once raise a suspicion that they may have been copied from military uniforms. While we have found no specific evidence to support such a view, its great probability must be recognized. On the other hand, the placing of these bands over the seams of the older shirts takes us back to a principle of decoration used on other parts of aboriginal costume and therefore is strong argument for the aboriginal origin of the bands, though it may well be that military models modified them later. We find upon a number of shirts a secondary fringed band covering the seam where the sleeve is attached and again in cases where the slanting long bands are absent we often find the short fringed band over this seam. This would be consistent with the military origin of the slanting band.

According to tradition, the hair fringe had a definite function among the Dakota but it is not certain that the decoration originated among them. However, the concealing of seams by fringes of skin and other materials was common, as will be noted on other men's garments illustrated in the preceding paper. In distribution this method of concealing seams by fringes seems to have been the prevailing mode in northern United States as far west as the Coast Salish and gave us the characteristic coat of the white trapper. The fact that both the bands and the fringes follow the seams leads us to the conclusion that their position and place was determined by the structure of the garment.

There is still another curious decorative feature to these shirts. The most of them have at the throat and back of the neck a triangular pendant, usually highly decorated. This cannot be accounted for on structural grounds for it has no necessary part in forming the garment nor does it conceal any defect. It cannot be the tail for this is at the bottom of the shirt. In Carver's book (p. 230) we have an illustration of a Dakota (?) wearing no upper garment, but at his throat is hung a triangular object which in form and design suggests the pendant upon these shirts. From the text we see that this is a knife sheath.

The dagger placed near it in the same plate, is peculiar to the Naudowessie nation, and of ancient construction, but they can give no account how long it has been in use among them. It was originally made of flint or bone, but since they have had communication with the European traders, they have formed it of steel. The length of it is about ten inches, and that part close to the handle nearly three inches broad. Its edges are keen, and it gradually tapers towards a point. They wear it in a sheath made of deer's leather, neatly ornamented with porcupines quills; and it is usually hung by a string, decorated in the same manner, which reaches as low only as the breast. This curious weapon is worn by a few of the principal chiefs alone, and considered both as a useful instrument, and an ornamental badge of superiority.[1]

Now while this does not prove that the triangular ornament upon Plains shirts was derived from the conventional knife sheath badge of office, it does nevertheless offer one rational explanation. In the discussion of distribu-

Fig. 2 (50–4516b).   Blackfoot Mcccasin Decoration and Pattern.   The sole and upper are in one piece.

tion of these shirts (vol. 5, p. 135) we have shown reasons for assuming the type to have been dispersed from the Dakota. Also, it is here that we find this shirt to have been the badge of high office in the tribe (vol. 11, p. 7). Hence, what is said about the conventional knife sheath is consistent with this. Further speculation on this point is unnecessary, but some field inquiry might be worth while. Not all these pendants are triangular, some being rectangular, but the triangular one is the most frequent and most widely distributed.

---

[1] Carver, John, *Travels through the Interior Parts of North America*, London, 1778, 296.

MOCCASIN DECORATIONS.

In order to give our studies of ornamentation a broader foundation we extended them to moccasin decorations. One of the first interesting cases is the U-shaped design on Blackfoot moccasins (Fig. 2). The structures of these moccasins have been discussed in vol. 5, p. 140,[1] but we see from the figure that the sole and upper are in one piece. The design is not placed directly upon the upper, but upon a red cloth which is then sewed down upon the leather. Such designs are very frequent on Blackfoot moccasins and are by tradition the older style. Fig. 3 reproduced from vol. 5 shows a similar design upon a hard-soled moccasin. Another variant of the design is shown in Fig. 4. In both cases the design is beaded upon red cloth as before and then sewed down upon the leather.

Now the question arises as to what suggested this peculiar overlay ornamentation which has no visible function in the structure. Of the immediate neighbors of the Blackfoot only the Sarsi, Assiniboin, and Northern Shoshoni have so far been observed to make occasional use of this style, but farther east and north we find it of frequent occurrence. Examples have been illustrated by Mr. Skinner in vol. 9, pp. 20 and 123, Figs. 6 and 41, and also in vol. 5, p. 144, Fig. 91 (reproduced here as Fig. 5). From the descriptions in these references, we see that here in contrast to the Blackfoot we have a structural relation between the U-shaped design and the moccasin pattern. The pattern required an insert of this shape to which the gathered edge of the upper gives a bold contour. On many of the moccasins from the Cree and Montagnais, around Hudson's Bay, this insert is covered with cloth, usually red or dark blue. On others, the insert is of leather but it bears the decorations, while the remainder of the upper is plain. This general pattern with a U-shaped insert is very common among the Cree, Saulteaux, Montagnais, Naskapi, Déné, Thompson, Shuswap, and a few random specimens have been noted among the Crow and Shoshoni.

Now, returning to the Blackfoot we see that they differ from all these tribes only in that the decoration is upon a different moccasin pattern. The pattern they use does not require an insert, so in order to follow the same style they make a false one. Here we can have no doubt as to who are the imitators.

---

[1] A far more exhaustive study of the subject has been made by Dr. Gudmund Hatt in, *Mokkasiner geografisk Tidsskrift,* 22 B. H. V. Copenhagen, 1914; 172–182; *Arktiske Skinddragter,* Copenhagen, 1914, 168–172, and who is about to publish an even more detailed discussion in English.

Another interesting problem is as to whether the Blackfoot have changed the structure of their moccasins or simply borrowed a style of decoration. The distribution may throw some light upon this point.   So far, the structural pattern of the Blackfoot moccasin (Fig. 2) is found among the Western Cree, Thompson, Nez Percé, Sarsi, Assiniboin, Gros Ventre, and Northern

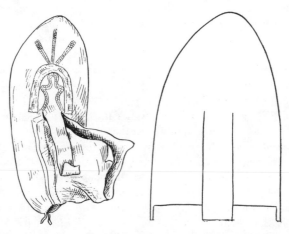

Fig. 3 (50–4566).   Blackfoot Moccasin with Hard Sole, but Decorated as in Fig. 2. The upper is a separate piece of skin.

Fig. 4 (50–4406).   Blackfoot Moccasin of Hard-soled Pattern with Decoration similar to Fig. 2.

Shoshoni.   It is therefore a localized type in contradistinction to the insert pattern of the east.   But curiously enough, only the Blackfoot and the small tribes under their influence have this decoration well developed.   The chances then favor their having borrowed the pattern and substituted it for one of the eastern type, but retaining the old style of decoration.   They also took over the hard sole type of moccasin typical of the Plains and in many cases placed the decoration upon it as well (Fig. 3).   There is in fact a close similarity between the structures of Blackfoot one-piece moccasins we have just described and those of the hard sole type, for when we compare them with the eastern insert type, we see that the former have the common concept of an upper and a sole.   One may suspect therefore that

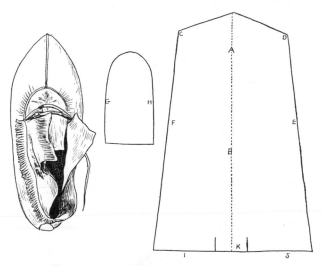

Fig. 5 (1–4614).   Type Pattern for Moccasin with U-shaped Insert.   For details of structure see vol. 5, p. 144.

this one-piece pattern was developed by a people familiar with hard sole moccasins.   Thus we have here another instance of an intermediate structural type occupying an area between two other areas of contrasting types (p. 89).

We may turn to another style of moccasin decoration in the Plains, a simple band over the top.   It takes two general forms as in Fig. 6.   In our collections form *a* (the first five) occurs among the Blackfoot, Sarsi, Gros Ventre, Arapaho, Assiniboin, and *b* (the sixth and seventh) among the Cheyenne, Crow, Dakota, and Arapaho.   In every case it is found on moccasins of the two-piece pattern and occupies the middle of an un-

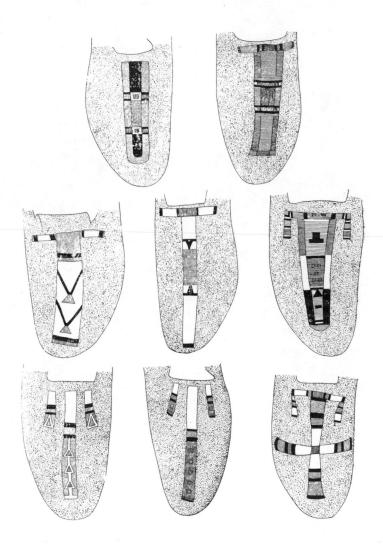

Fig. 6 (1–5709, 50–583, 50–1021, 50–585, 50–410, 1–5707, 50–582, 50–584).   Arapaho Moccasins bearing the Banded-Upper Type of Decorations.   From Bulletin vol. 18, plate I.

broken surface. There is, therefore, no structural relation such as we
found in some eastern moccasins. Yet, when we look outside of the Plains
area we find a similar band used to conceal an unsightly puckered seam.
This is particularly true of Iroquois moccasins but also occurs on those of
the Kickapoo, Sauk, Fox, Penobscot, and Delaware. A type specimen

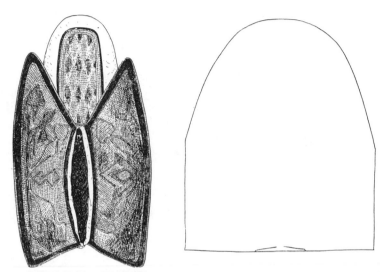

Fig. 7 (50–2263). A Sauk Moccasin with Overlay Decoration. A single piece of skin
folded over the foot so a˜ to form a seam on the instep.

Fig. 8 (50–7557). Winnebago Moccasin with Top Fringe and Beaded Band Decoration.

is shown in Fig. 7. Usually the beaded or quilled designs are upon a strip of leather which is sewed down upon the moccasin.

Thus we have another case quite analogous to the preceding but one in which the evidence for a historical relation is far less convincing. Nevertheless, the selection of this style by the Iroquois, for example, is clearly an adjustment to the pattern and offers one more example of the structural control of costume decoration. The use of the same style in the Plains in disassociation from the pattern may prove to be a case of convergent evolution but the probability of its structural origin cannot be denied.

A special variation of this pattern is noted in the Winnebago specimen, Fig. 8. Here a fringe is placed on the seam between two narrow beaded bands. Among the Teton-Dakota we find the decoration produced upon a two-piece moccasin by sewing down the fringe into the beadwork (Fig. 9).

One more problem in moccasin decoration may be cited. Among the Apache we find a curious pattern for the upper of a hard sole moccasin, Fig. 10. A slit is cut almost the full length of the upper and a long V-shaped piece inserted. Just why this is done is not clear but the result is two long seams terminating in a point. It is barely possible that the originators of this moccasin were familiar with the pattern in Fig. 5 and carried over the idea of an upper insert when adopting the hard sole two-piece pattern, but there is as yet no very good evidence in support of this.

Many moccasins of this pattern are undecorated save for a fringe on one side of the insert. The insert itself is often painted red, blue or yellow. When beads are added we find a border down each of the seams usually joining the border skirting the sole. This gives us a characteristic style of decoration in which two converging lines extend down the top of the upper (Fig. 11).

Fig. 9 (50–5221). A Hard-soled Moccasin with Median Fringe upon the Upper. Dakota. In this case the fringe is sewed down upon an even surface. Pattern same as Fig. 3.

The Apache pattern is found among the Comanche and occasionally among the Kiowa but the style of decoration has been observed among the Cheyenne, Arapaho, Crow, Dakota, Assiniboin, Blackfoot, and Gros Ventre. In most cases the converging bands are placed upon the upper of a simple two-piece pattern as in Fig. 11b, but occasionally a fringe is added and the enclosed V-shaped space painted. Since we find a continuous distribution of this style and all degrees of association between it and the essential structural features, the most acceptable explanation of the case is that the style of decoration developed on moccasins of the Apache pattern. Of course, this does not imply that the Apache were the originators.

We have now examined three styles of moccasin decoration in the Plains area and in each case found good reasons for assuming their development as due to the structural type of the original moccasin. While in the second case cited it may be that the style was independently developed in the Plains

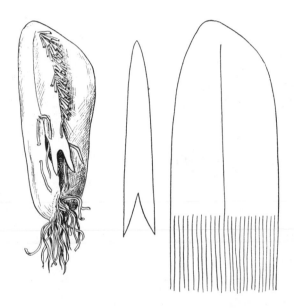

Fig. 10 (1–5423). An Apache Moccasin. The long tongue-like insert is usually painted and frequently bordered by beaded bands.

area, it is clear that in the east its use grew out of the structural concept. Since we have also found this principle to operate in body clothing in the same areas, a very important problem is presented. We must in the future give more consideration to the principle of survivals in style to the extent of transferring particular styles to new structural patterns. It does not follow though, that wherever we find the style upon a foreign pattern, the pattern has been changed. Thus, in case of the third type of moccasin decoration we have discussed, there is no reason to doubt but that the style was diffused more widely than the structural pattern. This part of our investigation suggests that the further development of these problems in the Plains area may forge a new link in the chain of evidence for former historical connections.

In connection with dress decorations we found an interesting point in the symbolic associations of certain designs. A similar relation appears in certain moccasin decorations. A moccasin was collected from the

Fig. 11 (50–658a, 50.1–6339a). A Decorated Apache Moccasin and a Simple Two-piece Moccasin from the Arapaho, bearing the same style of decoration.

Dakota in the third style as described above (Fig. 12). In this case the beaded bands were in white and were said to represent the warpath in winter. Considering all that has gone before it is impossible to conclude that the placing of the bands in this way was first hit upon by an individual who wished to represent a warpath covered with snow.

The U-shaped design among the Blackfoot seems to have no definite symbolic associates but the maker of Fig. 3 said that the three radiating lines and the curved border represented the aurora and the human figure, the "white men of the north dancing." (The Blackfoot belief is that some white-colored men reside in the far north and that the aurora is their dance fire.) This appeared to be an individual interpretation but still is an example of the secondary use of a style of decoration in the expression of a mythical idea. In this case we can see just how much the maker may have originated, but since the same figures were made by others (Fig. 4) we must doubt that even here the maker did anything more than read into the conventional pattern.

Fig. 12 (50–2993b). Symbolic Decoration upon Teton Moccasin of the Apache Style. The pattern is that of Fig. 3.

CONCLUDING REMARKS.

The preceding discussion does not consider the detailed design but only the decorated units of surface. For data upon this point we checked over the large series of moccasins in our collections. While the small figures used in the bands and fields of decoration are very widely diffused over the area, we failed to find that the style of decoration influenced the choice of them. Elaborate designs are unsuitable because of their large size but beyond this there seem to have been no limitations to their use. The two-piece moccasin of the Plains with its broad unbroken expanse of upper encouraged more elaborate designs than the patterns of the east. In the latter region the ankle flaps and sometimes an enlarged tongue were taken as the decorative surfaces, thus giving an entirely different objective aspect. But aside from the mere difference in the size of the decorative fields and the influence of the local modes of artistic expression, we have found no correlation between these styles and the design detail.

The method we have followed in these investigations differs from that formerly employed in that we have not based our conclusions upon objective resemblances but upon the correlations of such resemblances and facts of culture distribution. Thus the reader may object to our interpretation of the resemblances by which we group moccasin styles in Fig. 11 on the ground that we have simply selected from a large number of moccasins those that happened to resemble the chosen type. In this case the underlying assumption would probably be that the whole was merely an accident of variation in moccasin decoration.   The correlations we have cited have an important bearing here.   The style of decoration carries three rather distinct units between which there appears no necessary association; the converging narrow lines, the painted space, and the fringe.   The tendency of these to appear together in the Plains complicates the accidental interpretation. Then the distribution shows this style to prevail among these tribes using the corresponding structural pattern of moccasins, while its appearance elsewhere upon the two-piece moccasin is but occasional.   Finally, the distribution of these random examples is geographically continuous with the tribes using the corresponding structural patterns and relatively restricted.   It is such correlations as these that we have appealed to for guidance in our interpretations.